C000000255

BE STRONG

KIND WORDS FOR DIFFICULT TIMES

BE STRONG

An Hachette UK Company
www.hachette.co.uk

Vie Books, an imprint of Summersdale Publishers Ltd
Part of Octopus Publishing Group Limited
Carmelite House
50 Victoria Embankment
LONDON
EC4Y 0DZ
UK

www.summersdale.com

Printed and bound in the Czech Republic

ISBN: 978-1-78783-996-0

Substantial discounts on bulk quantities of Summersdale books are available to corporations, professional associations and other organizations. For details contact general enquiries: telephone: +44 (0) 1243 771107 or email: enquiries@summersdale.com.

Love your flaws.
Own your quirks.
And know that you
are just as perfect
as anyone else,
exactly as you are.

ARIANA GRANDE

To ....

From ....

Nerves just mean that you care.

EVAN PETERS

YOU ARE
AMAZING
IN EVERY
SINGLE WAY

You only get one

CHANCE

at life and you

HAVE TO

grab it boldly.

BEAR GRYLLS

DON'T TRY TO FIT IN.
STAND OUT.
STAND STRONG.

DIANDRA FORREST

Owning your story
is the bravest thing
you will ever do.

BRENÉ BROWN

YOU ARE POSITIVELY AWESOME

If you're walking
down the right path
and you're willing
to keep walking,
eventually you'll
make progress.

BARACK OBAMA

I CAN BE CHANGED
BY WHAT
HAPPENS TO ME.
BUT I REFUSE TO BE
REDUCED BY IT.

MAYA ANGELOU

You have to believe
in yourself when
no one else does –
that makes you a
winner right there.

VENUS WILLIAMS

SEIZE
THE
DAY

You mustn't
confuse a
single failure
with a
final defeat.

F. SCOTT FITZGERALD

We must not allow other people's limited perceptions to define us.

VIRGINIA SATIR

PUT YOUR MIND TO IT AND YOU CAN ACCOMPLISH ANYTHING

Faith is taking the first step, even when you don't see the whole staircase.

MARTIN LUTHER KING JR

I want to

EMBRACE

my full self, as

NATURAL

as I can be.

WILLOW SMITH

PERSEVERANCE
IS THE KEY
TO SUCCESS

Sometimes it all
gets a little too much,
but you gotta realize that
soon the fog will clear up.

SHAWN MENDES

YOUR VICTORY IS
RIGHT AROUND
THE CORNER.
NEVER GIVE UP.

NICKI MINAJ

I learned
that courage
was not the
absence of
fear, but
the triumph
over it.

NELSON MANDELA

PUSH YOUR BOUNDARIES

You cannot make
a difference unless
you're different.

JUSTIN TIMBERLAKE

Just be yourself,
be you, and
don't be afraid to
speak your mind.

CHLOË GRACE MORETZ

DON'T LET ANYONE HOLD YOU BACK

The most difficult thing
is the decision to act.
The rest is merely tenacity.

AMELIA EARHART

Power for
me is "no"...
That's when you
know your worth,
when you know
your value.

TARAJI P. HENSON

Your struggles

DEVELOP

your strengths.

ARNOLD SCHWARZENEGGER

IT'S OK
NOT TO BE OK

POSITIVITY,
CONFIDENCE AND
PERSISTENCE ARE
KEY IN LIFE,
SO NEVER GIVE UP
ON YOURSELF.

KHALID

Every flower blooms at a different pace.

SUZY KASSEM

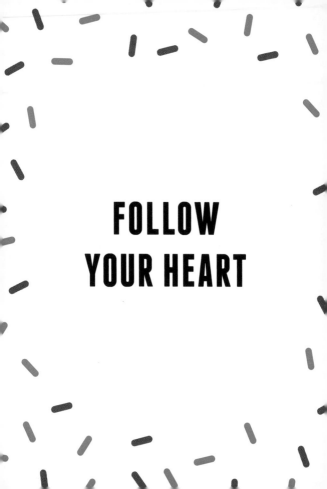

FOLLOW
YOUR HEART

You never know how strong you are, until being strong is your only choice.

BOB MARLEY

Let your dreams push you...
instead of your fears.

ZARA HAIRSTON

If you don't try
things and take risks,
you don't really
grow and figure out
what you want.

ZENDAYA

SETBACKS HAPPEN TO EVERYONE: IT'S HOW YOU DEAL WITH THEM THAT COUNTS

SPEAK UP.
BELIEVE IN
YOURSELF.
TAKE RISKS.

SHERYL SANDBERG

Sometimes the
smallest step in the
right direction ends up
being the biggest
step of your life.

NAEEM CALLAWAY

LIVE LIFE WITH PURPOSE

Don't you ever let a soul in the world tell you that you can't be exactly who you are.

LADY GAGA

There's

ALWAYS

a way.

BRITNEY SPEARS

I love finding
things that scare
me and doing them.
That's how you grow.

VANESSA HUDGENS

DON'T BE AFRAID TO MAKE MISTAKES

Be yourself...
it really doesn't matter what other people think.

TAYLOR SCHILLING

You're strong.
You're a Kelly
Clarkson song.
You've got this.

JONATHAN VAN NESS

NEVER
GIVE UP

DOUBT WHOM
YOU WILL,
BUT NEVER
YOURSELF.

CHRISTIAN NESTELL BOVEE

Happiness and confidence
are the prettiest things
you can wear.

TAYLOR SWIFT

The whole point is
to live life and be –
to use all the colours
in the crayon box.

RuPAUL

YOU WERE BORN TO BE REAL – NOT PERFECT

Your self-worth
is determined
by you.
You don't have
to depend on
someone telling
you who you are.

BEYONCÉ

Life happens. Adapt.
Embrace change,
and make the most
of everything that
comes your way.

NICK JONAS

BE THE PERSON YOU TRULY WANT TO BE

Courage is

FOUND

in unlikely

PLACES.

J. R. R. TOLKIEN

Courage doesn't always roar. Sometimes courage is the quiet voice at the end of the day saying, "I will try again tomorrow."

MARY ANNE RADMACHER

I don't want the
fear of failure
to stop me from
doing what I
really care about.

EMMA WATSON

YOU'RE ALLOWED TO SCREAM. YOU'RE ALLOWED TO CRY. BUT DO NOT GIVE UP.

STAY FOCUSED.
BE CONSISTENT
AND
YOU'LL SUCCEED.

RYAN REYNOLDS

You can be the lead
in your own life.

KERRY WASHINGTON

YOU DON'T HAVE TO LOOK STRONG TO BE STRONG

The most important thing, in anything you do, is always trying your hardest.

TOM HOLLAND

HARD WORK AND
AMBITION
CAN TAKE YOU A
LONG WAY.

DWAYNE JOHNSON

There's always tomorrow
and it always gets better!

ARIANA GRANDE

DON'T LIVE IN FEAR; WHEN DID THE WORST-CASE SCENARIO LAST HAPPEN TO YOU?

STORM?

Shine your

LIGHT

and make a rainbow.

RICHIE NORTON

Courage is
very important.
Like a muscle,
it is strengthened
by use.

RUTH GORDON

SOMETIMES STRENGTH IS HIDDEN WITHIN US; YOU JUST NEED TO DIG A LITTLE TO FIND IT

Being negative
only makes a difficult
journey more difficult.
You may be given a
cactus, but you don't
have to sit on it.

JOYCE MEYER

Three in the
morning is
never the time
to try and sort
out your life.

MATT HAIG

WHEN YOU FIND
YOUR PATH,
YOU MUST
NOT BE AFRAID.

PAULO COELHO

BRAVERY
COMES WHEN
YOU BELIEVE
IN YOURSELF

Be sure what you want and be sure about yourself... You have to believe in yourself and be strong.

ADRIANA LIMA

Fear is only as

DEEP

as the mind

ALLOWS.

JAPANESE PROVERB

YOU ARE CAPABLE OF ANYTHING

Know that you are
not stuck where you are
unless you decide to be.

WAYNE W. DYER

The way you
carry yourself is
influenced by the
way you feel inside.

MARILYN MONROE

Everything you've ever wanted is sitting on the other side of fear.

GEORGE ADDAIR

BE PROUD
OF WHO
YOU ARE

YOU MUST DO
THE THING
YOU THINK
YOU CANNOT DO.

ELEANOR ROOSEVELT

Don't

HIDE

from who you are.

RIHANNA

SHOW YOURSELF THE SAME RESPECT YOU SHOW TO OTHERS

Anyone can hide.
Facing up to
things, working
through them,
that's what
makes you strong.

SARAH DESSEN

You never know how
the tough times you are
going through today
will inspire someone
else tomorrow.

TIM TEBOW

Where there is no struggle,
there is no strength.

OPRAH WINFREY

YOU

GOT

THIS

SELF-TRUST

IS THE FIRST

SECRET

TO SUCCESS.

RALPH WALDO EMERSON

Believe in yourself and you will be able to move mountains.

BINDI IRWIN

**TURN YOUR
FEARS INTO
POSITIVE
ENERGY**

WORK

hard and

SUCCESS

will follow.

TOM DALEY

I thrive on
obstacles.
If I'm told that it
can't be done,
then I push harder.

ISSA RAE

If you're making
mistakes it means
you're out there
doing something.

NEIL GAIMAN

LOOK AFTER
YOURSELF

It's about being who you are. If people can't accept it, too bad.

KYLIE JENNER

I DON'T
KNOW WHAT
CHAPTER
I'M ON.
I ONLY KNOW
WHERE I AM.

TIMOTHÉE CHALAMET

FEEL YOUR FEELINGS

You can't really be strong until you can see a funny side to things.

KEN KESEY

Life is very interesting.
In the end, some
of your greatest
pains become your
greatest strengths.

DREW BARRYMORE

I'VE ALWAYS
BELIEVED THAT
YOU SHOULD
NEVER, EVER
GIVE UP.

MICHAEL SCHUMACHER

LIVE IN
THE MOMENT

The difference between
winning and losing is most
often not quitting.

WALT DISNEY

A hero is
an ordinary
individual who
finds the strength
to persevere and
endure in spite
of overwhelming
obstacles.

CHRISTOPHER REEVE

CELEBRATE
SMALL VICTORIES

The people who put you down don't have to stop you from chasing your dreams. Stand up and prove them wrong.

SELENA GOMEZ

We need

COURAGE.

AMAL CLOONEY

Don't block your blessings. Don't let doubt stop you from getting where you want to be.

JENNIFER HUDSON

WORRY LESS,
LIVE MORE

Most of the important things in the world have been accomplished by people who have kept on trying when there seemed to be no hope at all.

DALE CARNEGIE

I don't believe in luck...
It's persistence,
hard work and not
forgetting your dream.

JANET JACKSON

BEING BRAVE CONSISTS OF TAKING SMALL STEPS

All things are

POSSIBLE.

AMANDLA STENBERG

BE FEARLESS,
BE BRAVE,
BE BOLD,
LOVE YOURSELF.

HARUKI MURAKAMI

You have
to believe
in yourself
when no one
else does.

SERENA WILLIAMS

REMOVE "REGRET" FROM YOUR VOCABULARY

The lessons learned
when I don't win
only strengthen me.

LEWIS HAMILTON

I'D RATHER
BE LOUD AND
MISUNDERSTOOD
THAN QUIET
AND BORED.

ADAM LEVINE

THINK POSITIVE, BE POSITIVE

You are allowed
to be both a
masterpiece and a
work in progress,
simultaneously.

SOPHIA BUSH

It's not always
necessary
to be strong,
but to feel strong.

JON KRAKAUER

You gain confidence
by doing things
before you're ready,
while you're still scared.

ELLEN HENDRIKSEN

LIFE IS YOURS
FOR THE TAKING

We all start somewhere.
It's where you end
up that counts.

RIHANNA

Within you there is a stillness and sanctuary to which you can retreat at any time and be yourself.

HERMANN HESSE

NEVER STOP
PURSUING
YOUR DREAMS

YOU BUILD
ON FAILURE.
YOU USE IT AS A
STEPPING STONE.

JOHNNY CASH

Bravery is to

STAND UP

for what

YOU

believe in.

SOPHIE TURNER

I think that the most beautiful thing a human being can do is just be who you are inside.

JOSH HUTCHERSON

WORRIES ARE MADE UP; DON'T LET THEM ENTER YOUR REALITY

When you feel
out of your depth,
breathe and
keep moving.

CHARLIE MACKESY

I know the sun will
rise in the morning,
that there is a light at the
end of every tunnel.

MICHAEL MORPURGO

YOU ARE SO AWESOME

Strength is the ability to break a chocolate bar into four pieces with your bare hands – and then eat just one of those pieces.

JUDITH VIORST

YOU DESERVE
GREATNESS,
SO GIVE IT TO
YOURSELF.

CHIDERA EGGERUE

Freedom

LIES

in being

BOLD.

ROBERT FROST

YOUR DIFFERENCES ARE WHAT MAKE YOU UNIQUE; CELEBRATE THEM

Make bold choices
and make mistakes.
It's all those things
that add up to the
person you become.

ANGELINA JOLIE

At any given
moment you have
the power to say:
This is not how
the story is
going to end.

CHRISTINE MASON MILLER

LET NOTHING
HOLD YOU BACK

LIFE SHRINKS
OR EXPANDS
ACCORDING TO
ONE'S COURAGE.

ANAÏS NIN

There will be obstacles.
There will be doubters.
There will be mistakes.
But with hard work...
there are no limits.

MICHAEL PHELPS

Never say never, because limits, like fears, are often just an illusion.

MICHAEL JORDAN

BE KIND
TO YOURSELF

You can do whatever
you really love to do,
no matter what it is.

RYAN GOSLING

It's only when you
risk failure that
you discover things.

LUPITA NYONG'O

DON'T LIVE IN THE PAST; KEEP MOVING FORWARD

To accomplish
great things,
we must
not only act,
but also dream;
not only plan,
but also believe.

ANATOLE FRANCE

You have to be able to love yourself because that's when things fall into place.

VANESSA HUDGENS

THE TESTS OF LIFE
ARE NOT MEANT
TO BREAK YOU,
BUT TO MAKE YOU.

NORMAN VINCENT PEALE

FAILURE IS
A STEPPING
STONE TO
BUILDING
STRENGTH

Impossible only means
that you haven't found
the solution yet.

ANONYMOUS

Owning up to

YOUR

vulnerabilities is a

FORM

of strength.

LIZZO

RESPECTING
WHEREVER YOU
FIND YOURSELF IS
GOOD ENOUGH.

COLIN FARRELL

If you do not
care for yourself,
you will not be
strong enough
to take care of
anything in life.

LEON BROWN

THERE IS
NO ONE
LIKE YOU

Just don't give up
trying to do what you
really want to do.

ELLA FITZGERALD

I'd rather regret the risks that didn't work out than the chances I didn't take at all.

SIMONE BILES

**Look up,
laugh loud,
talk big,
keep the colour
in your cheek
and the fire in
your eye.**

WILLIAM HAZLITT

BE STRONG

Have you enjoyed this book?
If so, find us on Facebook at
Summersdale Publishers, on Twitter
at @Summersdale and on Instagram
at @summersdalebooks and get in
touch. We'd love to hear from you!

www.summersdale.com